GILGAMESH

A VERSE NARRATIVE

GILGAMESH

A VERSE NARRATIVE

Herbert Mason

A MARINER BOOK

HOUGHTON MIFFLIN COMPANY

Boston • New York

FIRST MARINER BOOKS EDITION 2003

Library of Congress Cataloging-in-Publication Data

Mason, Herbert, date.
    Gilgamesh : a verse narrative / Herbert Mason. —
1st Mariner Books ed.
    p. cm.
    "A Mariner book."
    ISBN-13: 978-0-618-27564-9 (pbk.)
    ISBN-10: 0-618-27564-9 (pbk.)
    1. Erech (Extinct city) — Kings and rulers — Poetry.
2. Epic poetry, Assyro-Babylonian — Adaptations. 3. Epic
poetry, American. I. Gilgamesh. II. Title.

    PS3563.A7923G5 2003
    811'.54 — dc21   2003050853

Printed in the United States of America

DOC 25 24 23 22   4500736233

A portion of this book appeared in *The American Scholar*.

Contents

GILGAMESH

A VERSE NARRATIVE

It is an old story
But one that can still be told
About a man who loved
And lost a friend to death
And learned he lacked the power
To bring him back to life.
It is the story of Gilgamesh
And his friend Enkidu.

I

Gilgamesh was king of Uruk,
A city set between the Tigris
And Euphrates rivers
In ancient Babylonia.
Enkidu was born on the Steppe
Where he grew up among the animals.
Gilgamesh was called a god and man;
Enkidu was an animal and man.
It is the story
Of their becoming human together.

As king, Gilgamesh was a tyrant to his people.
He demanded, from an old birthright,
The privilege of sleeping with their brides
Before the husbands were permitted.

Sometimes he pushed his people half to death
With work rebuilding Uruk's walls,
And then without an explanation let
The walls go unattended and decay,
And left his people dreaming of the past
And longing for a change.
They had grown tired of his contradictions
And his callous ways.
They knew his world was old
And cluttered with spoiled arts
That they defended but could not revive.

Enkidu was ignorant of oldness.
He ran with the animals,
Drank at their springs,
Not knowing fear or wisdom.
He freed them from the traps
The hunters set.

A hunter's son one day
Saw Enkidu opening a trap:
The creature was all covered with hair
And yet his hands had the dexterity of men's;
He ran beside the freed gazelle
Like a brother
And they drank together at a pool
Like two friends
Sharing some common journey
Not needing to speak but just continue.

Gilgamesh was a godlike man alone
With his thoughts in idleness except
For those evenings when he went down

Into the marketplace to the Family House
To sleep with the virgins, or when
He told his dreams to his mother, Ninsun.

The hunter listened to his son's
Description of Enkidu
And was both angry and afraid.
He told his son to go to Uruk
And to tell what he had seen
To Gilgamesh and to ask him
To send a prostitute
Who would sleep with Enkidu
And make the animals ashamed of him.
Gilgamesh would understand, for he was king.

The hunter's son made the day's journey
To Uruk and told what he had seen
To Gilgamesh, showing him
His father's anger and his fear
And praising the strength of the strange
Creature who had come to his father's plains
And freed the animals from the traps
And lived as one of them
And threatened the livelihood of men.
Gilgamesh listened but he had heard
So many stories of the Wondrous
Creatures of the Forest and the Steppe
That he could hardly be aroused.
He sent the prostitute but then forgot
What he had listened to.

The hunter left the prostitute alone
At the spring. When evening came,

Enkidu appeared among the animals
And drank with them and rested at their side.
When he awoke he saw a creature
Unlike any he had seen before
Standing near the water, its skin smooth, tan
And hairless except for its head
And between its legs.
He wanted to touch it, but then
It made sounds he had never heard,
Not like the sounds of his friends, the animals,
And he was afraid. The prostitute
Came close to him and the animals withdrew.
She took his hand and guided it
Across her breasts and between her legs
And touched him with her fingers
Gently and bent down and moistened
Him with her lips then drew him
Slowly to the ground.

When he rose again
Looking for his friends who had gone,
He felt a strange exhaustion,
As if life had left his body.
He felt their absence.
He imagined the gazelles raising the dry dust
Like soft brush floating on the crests of sand
Swiftly changing direction, and the serpents
Asleep at the springs, slipping effortlessly
Into the water, and the wild she-camel
Vanishing into the desert. His friends
Had left him to a vast aloneness
He had never felt before. The lions returned
To the mountains, the water buffalo
To the rivers, the birds to the sky.

Gilgamesh woke anxiously from a dream
And said to Ninsun: I saw a star
Fall from the sky, and the people
Of Uruk stood around and admired it,
And I was jealous and tried to carry it away
But I was too weak and I failed.
What does it mean? I have not dreamed
Like this before.

She said: Your equal is the star
Which fell, as if a sign from Heaven
Had been sent which is too heavy
But which you will try to lift
And drive away, and fail.

But I have never failed before, he interrupted
Her, surprised himself at his anxiety.
It will be a person, she continued,
Speaking in her somber monotone,
A companion who is your equal
In strength, a person loyal to a friend,
Who will not forsake you and whom you
Will never wish to leave.

Gilgamesh was quiet at this interpretation
Of his dream.

That night he had a vision of an ax.
What does this mean, he said on waking;
The people stood around the ax
When I tried to lift it, and I failed.
I feel such tiredness. I cannot explain.

19

Ninsun said: The ax is a man
Who is your friend and equal.
He will come. A graceful man
Who will lift you out of tiredness.

O Ninsun, I want your words to be true.
I have never known such weariness before,
As if some life in me has disappeared
Or needs to be filled up again.
I am alone and I have longed
For some companionship. My people
Also have grown tired of my solitude.

∽

The prostitute slept beside Enkidu
Until he was used to her body.
She knew how gradually one stops
Desiring to run with old companions.
One morning she awoke and said to him:
Why do you still want to run with the animals?
You are a human being now, not like them.
You are like a god, like Gilgamesh.
I will lead you to Uruk
Where you belong, to the Temple of Anu
Where Gilgamesh rules over his people
And is strong, and you will recognize
Yourself in him, as in a clear stream
You see your own face, a man's face.
He listened to her words
And to the unfamiliar names
Of Anu, Gilgamesh . . . and he felt weak.
He let her clothe him in a portion

Of her scarlet robe and lead him
To a shepherd's house
Where he was welcomed and taught to eat bread
And drink the liquor that the shepherds drank.
His soul felt new and strange
And his face was hot with sweat
And somehow gay. The prostitute
Shaved the long hair off his body;
She washed him with perfumes and oils,
And he became a man. At night
He stood watch for the shepherds
Against the lions so they could sleep,
He captured wolves for them,
And he was known as their Protector.

One day a man who was going to Uruk
Stopped to eat at the shepherd's house.
He told them he was hurrying to the marketplace
To choose for himself a virgin bride
Whom Gilgamesh by his birthright
Would sleep with before him.

Enkidu's face was pale.
He felt a weakness in his body
At the mention of their king.
He asked the prostitute
Why this should be his birthright.
She answered: He is king.

Enkidu entered Uruk.
The prostitute walked behind him.

The marketplace filled with people
When they heard that he was coming.
People said: He looks like Gilgamesh
But he is shorter and also stronger;
He has the power of the Steppe,
The milk of the animals he sucked.
They hailed him as the equal of their king.

At night when Gilgamesh approached
The market square to go into the Family House
Where the bride was to be chosen, Enkidu stood
Blocking his way. Gilgamesh looked at the stranger
And listened to his people's shouts of praise
For someone other than himself
And lunged at Enkidu.
They fell like wolves
At each other's throats,
Like bulls bellowing,
And horses gasping for breath
That have run all day
Desperate for rest and water,
Crushing the gate they fell against.
The dry dust billowed in the marketplace
And people shrieked. The dogs raced

In and out between their legs.
A child screamed at their feet
That danced the dance of life
Which hovers close to death.
And quiet suddenly fell on them
When Gilgamesh stood still
Exhausted. He turned to Enkidu who leaned
Against his shoulder and looked into his eyes
And saw himself in the other, just as Enkidu saw
Himself in Gilgamesh.
In the silence of the people they began to laugh
And clutched each other in their breathless exaltation.

II

Gilgamesh spoke then:
We go to kill the Evil One,
Humbaba. We must prove
Ourselves more powerful than he.

Enkidu was afraid of the forest of Humbaba
And urged him not to go, but he
Was not as strong as Gilgamesh in argument,
And they were friends:
They had embraced and made their vow
To stay together always,
No matter what the obstacle.
Enkidu tried to hold his fear

But he was sick at heart:
I feel the weakness that I felt before
Come over my body, as if I tried to lift
My arms and found that they were hollow.

It is Humbaba who has taken your strength,
Gilgamesh spoke out, anxious
For the journey. We must kill him
And end his evil power over us.

No, Enkidu cried; it is the journey
That will take away our life.

Don't be afraid, said Gilgamesh.
We are together. There is nothing
We should fear.

I learned, Enkidu said, when I lived
With the animals never to go down
Into *that* forest. I learned that there is death
In Humbaba. Why do you want
To raise his anger?

Only half listening Gilgamesh thought
Aloud about the cedars he would climb.

How can we climb those cedars?
Enkidu tried to sway his thoughts:
Humbaba never sleeps. He is the guardian
Whom Enlil has commanded to protect

The sacred trees by terror. I have learned
His sound is like a flood's sound
Slowly forming in the distance,
Then enveloping all other sounds.
Even the cries of animals cannot be heard.
Trees are hushed, the wind
Still moves them back and forth
But noiselessly. As when one senses
Violence gathering its force,
Soon there is no sound apart from it,
Not even one's own thoughts in terror.
I have learned that from his mouth springs fire
That scorches the earth and in a moment
There is nothing left alive,
No tree, no insect, as in a dream
That makes one wake and cry
Out of the pain one cannot find
The source of, out of nothing;
One wakes and everything has vanished.
I have learned Humbaba is the face of death.
He hears each insect crawling toward the edge
Of the forest; he twitches and it dies.
Do you think he could not hear two men?

Why are you worried about death?
Only the gods are immortal anyway,
Sighed Gilgamesh.
What men do is nothing, so fear is never
Justified. What happened to your power
That once could challenge and equal mine?
I will go ahead of you, and if I die
I will at least have the reward
Of having people say: He died in war

Against Humbaba. You cannot discourage me
With fears and hesitations.
I will fight Humbaba,
I will cut down his cedars.
Tell the armorers to build us two-edged swords
And double shields and tell them
I am impatient and cannot wait long.

Thus Gilgamesh and Enkidu went
Together to the marketplace
To notify the Elders of Uruk
Who were meeting in their senate.
They too were talking of Humbaba,
As they often did,
Edging always in their thoughts
Toward the forbidden.

The one you speak of, Gilgamesh addresssed them,
I now must meet. I want to prove
Him not the awesome thing we think he is
And that the boundaries set up by gods
Are not unbreakable. I will defeat him
In his cedar forest. The youth of Uruk
Need this fight. They have grown soft
And restless.

      The old men leaned a little forward
Remembering old wars. A flush burned on
Their cheeks. It seemed a little dangerous
And yet they saw their king
Was seized with passion for this fight.

Their voices gave the confidence his friend
Had failed to give; some even said
Enkidu's wisdom was a sign of cowardice.
You see, my friend, laughed Gilgamesh,
The wise of Uruk have outnumbered you.

Amidst the speeches in the hall
That called upon the gods for their protection,
Gilgamesh saw in his friend that pain
He had seen before and asked him what it was
That troubled him.

Enkidu could not speak. He held his tears
Back. Barely audibly he said:
It is a road which you have never traveled.

The armorers brought to Gilgamesh his weapons
And put them in his hand. He took his quiver,
Bow and ax, and two-edged sword,
And they began to march.

The Elders gave their austere blessing
And the people shouted: Let Enkidu lead,
Don't trust your strength, he knows the forests,
The one who goes ahead will save his friend.
May Shamash bring you victory.

Enkidu was resolved to lead his friend
Who was determined but did not know the way.
Now Gilgamesh was certain with his friend
Beside him. They went to Ninsun, his mother,
Who would advise them how to guard their steps.

Her words still filled his mind
As they started their journey,
Just as a mother's voice is heard
Sometimes in a man's mind
Long past childhood
Calling his name, calling him from sleep
Or from some pleasureful moment
On a foreign street
When every trace of origin seems left
And one has almost passed into a land
That promises a vision or the secret
Of one's life, when one feels almost god enough
To be free of voices, her voice
Calls out like a voice from childhood,
Reminding him he once tossed in dreams.

He still could smell the incense she had burned
To Shamash, saying: Why did you give my son
A restless heart, and now you touch him
With this passion to destroy Humbaba,
And you send him on a journey to a battle
He may never understand, to a door
He cannot open. You inspire him to end
The evil of the world which you abhor
And yet he is a man for all his power
And cannot do your work. You must protect
My son from danger.

              She had put out the incense
And called Enkidu to her side, and said:
You are not my son but I adopt you
And call upon the same protection now
For you I called upon for Gilgamesh.
She placed a charm around his neck, and said:
O let Enkidu now protect his friend.

These words still filled their minds
As the two friends continued on their way.

After three days they reached the edge
Of the forest where Humbaba's watchman stood.
Suddenly it was Gilgamesh who was afraid,
Enkidu who reminded him to be fearless.
The watchman sounded his warning to Humbaba.
The two friends moved slowly toward the forest gate.

When Enkidu touched the gate his hand felt numb,
He could not move his fingers or his wrist,
His face turned pale like someone's witnessing
                                    a death,
He tried to ask his friend for help
Whom he had just encouraged to move on,
But he could only stutter and hold out
His paralyzed hand.

It will pass, said Gilgamesh.
Would you want to stay behind because of that?
We must go down into the forest together.
Forget your fear of death. I will go before you
And protect you. Enkidu followed close behind
So filled with fear he could not think or speak.
Soon they reached the high cedars.

They stood in awe at the foot
Of the green mountain. Pleasure
Seemed to grow from fear for Gilgamesh.
As when one comes upon a path in woods
Unvisited by men, one is drawn near
The lost and undiscovered in himself;
He was revitalized by danger.
They knew it was the path Humbaba made.
Some called the forest "Hell," and others "Paradise";
What difference does it make? said Gilgamesh.
But night was falling quickly
And they had no time to call it names,
Except perhaps "The Dark,"
Before they found a place at the edge of the forest
To serve as shelter for their sleep.

It was a restless night for both. One snatched
At sleep and sprang awake from dreams. The other
Could not rest because of pain that spread
Throughout his side. Enkidu was alone
With sights he saw brought on by pain
And fear, as one in deep despair
May lie beside his love who sleeps
And seems so unafraid, absorbing in himself the
    phantoms
That she cannot see—phantoms diminished for one
When two can see and stay awake to talk of them
And search out a solution to despair,
Or lie together in each other's arms,
Or weep and in exhaustion from their tears
Perhaps find laughter for their fears.
But alone and awake the size and nature
Of the creatures in his mind grow monstrous,

36

Beyond resemblance to the creatures he had known
Before the prostitute had come into his life.
He cried aloud for them to stop appearing over him
Emerging from behind the trees with phosphorescent
    eyes
Brought on by rain. He could not hear his voice
But knew he screamed and could not move his arms
But thought they tried to move
As if a heavy weight he could not raise
Or wriggle out from underneath
Had settled on his chest,
Like a turtle trapped beneath a fallen branch,
Each effort only added to paralysis.
He could not make his friend, his one companion,
    hear.

Gilgamesh awoke but could not hear
His friend in agony, he still was captive to his dreams
Which he would tell aloud to exorcise:
I saw us standing in a mountain gorge,
A rockslide fell on us, we seemed no more
Than insects under it. And then
A solitary graceful man appeared
And pulled me out from under the mountain.
He gave me water and I felt released.

Tomorrow you will be victorious,
Enkidu said, to whom the dream brought chills
(For only one of them, he knew, would be released)
Which Gilgamesh could not perceive in the darkness
For he went back to sleep without responding
To his friend's interpretation of his dream.

Did you call me? Gilgamesh sat up again.
Why did I wake again? I thought you touched me.
Why am I afraid? I felt my limbs grow numb
As if some god passed over us drawing out our life.
I had another dream:
This time the heavens were alive with fire, but soon
The clouds began to thicken, death rained down on us,
The lightning flashes stopped, and everything
Which rained down turned to ashes.
What does this mean, Enkidu?

That you will be victorious against Humbaba,
Enkidu said, or someone said through him
Because he could not hear his voice
Or move his limbs although he thought he spoke,
And soon he saw his friend asleep beside him.

At dawn Gilgamesh raised his ax
And struck at the great cedar.
When Humbaba heard the sound of falling trees,
He hurried down the path that they had seen
But only he had traveled. Gilgamesh felt weak
At the sound of Humbaba's footsteps and called to
    Shamash
Saying, I have followed you in the way decreed;
Why am I abandoned now? Suddenly the winds
Sprang up. They saw the great head of Humbaba
Like a water buffalo's bellowing down the path,
His huge and clumsy legs, his flailing arms
Thrashing at phantoms in his precious trees.
His single stroke could cut a cedar down

And leave no mark on him. His shoulders,
Like a porter's under building stones,
Were permanently bent by what he bore;
He was the slave who did the work for gods
But whom the gods would never notice.
Monstrous in his contortion, he aroused
The two almost to pity.
But pity was the thing that might have killed.
It made them pause just long enough to show
How pitiless he was to them. Gilgamesh in horror saw
Him strike the back of Enkidu and beat him to the
    ground
Until he thought his friend was crushed to death.
He stood still watching as the monster leaned to make
His final strike against his friend, unable
To move to help him, and then Enkidu slid
Along the ground like a ram making its final lunge
On wounded knees. Humbaba fell and seemed
To crack the ground itself in two, and Gilgamesh,
As if this fall had snapped him from his daze,
Returned to life
And stood over Humbaba with his ax
Raised high above his head watching the monster plead
In strangled sobs and desperate appeals
The way the sea contorts under a violent squall.
I'll serve you as I served the gods, Humbaba said;
I'll build you houses from their sacred trees.

Enkidu feared his friend was weakening
And called out: Gilgamesh! Don't trust him!
As if there were some hunger in himself
That Gilgamesh was feeling
That turned him momentarily to yearn
For someone who would serve, he paused;
And then he raised his ax up higher

40

And swung it in a perfect arc
Into Humbaba's neck. He reached out
To touch the wounded shoulder of his friend,

And late that night he reached again
To see if he was yet asleep, but there was only
Quiet breathing. The stars against the midnight sky
Were sparkling like mica in a riverbed.
In the slight breeze
The head of Humbaba was swinging from a tree.

In the morning when they had bathed
And were preparing
To return to Uruk
Ishtar came,
Their city's patroness,
Goddess of love
And fruitfulness
And war.
She brought to Gilgamesh
His royal robes and crown
And hinted that the gods
Had grieved Humbaba's loss.
Why should *you* be chosen
As the one they blame?
She said in her coyness.
I might persuade

My father Anu to relent
If you marry me.
That is the way your kingdom
Will know peace.

Gilgamesh shook off what were to him
Unwanted dreams:
What would I gain by taking you as wife?

Love, she said, and peace.

Just as you loved the lion
And gave him pits to fall in
And the horse whose back
You wounded with the whip,
He shouted back at her.
Your love brings only war!
You are an old fat whore,
That's all you are,
Who once was beautiful,
Perhaps,
And could deceive
But who has left in men
A memory of grief.
We outgrow our naiveté
In thinking goddesses
Return our love.
I am tired of your promises,
Tired as Ishullanu,
Who brought you dates,
Innocent until you pressed

His hand against your breasts
And turned him to a mole
Who lived beneath
The surface of your earth,
Unable to dig out to air,
Feeling in his darkness
For that same soft touch.
He subsided in his insults
And turned away to his friend
Enkidu.

She stuttered she was so enraged
And flew to the protection of her father.

In his customary calm wise Anu noted that
Her sins had been declaimed this way before.
She shook in greater rage and said she had
No time to listen to reminders from old gods,
But only to ask him to make for her
The Bull of Heaven to destroy this man.
I will send him something
He would never wish to dream.
There will be more dead
Than living on this earth.
A drought that nothing will relieve.
He listened while her anger ran its course
And then reminded her: Men need
Survival after punishments.
Have you stored for them enough grain?
She knew her father's weakness for details
And said, I thought of that; they will not starve.
But a little hunger will replace
Their arrogance with new desire.

Then Anu acceded to her wish.
The Bull of Heaven descended
To the earth and killed at once
Three hundred men, and then attacked
King Gilgamesh.

                    Enkidu, to protect his friend,
Found strength. He lunged from side to side
Watching for his chance to seize the horns.
The bull frothed in its rage at this dance
And suddenly Enkidu seized its tail
And twisted it around, until the bull
Stood still, bewildered, out of breath,
And then Enkidu plunged his sword behind its horns
Into the nape of the bull's neck, and it fell dead.

The goddess stood on Uruk's walls, and cried aloud:
Grief to those who have insulted me
And killed the Bull of Heaven!

When Enkidu heard Ishtar's curse
He tore the right thigh from the bull's flesh
And hurled it in her face, and shouted:
I would tear you just like this
If I could catch you!
Then she withdrew among the prostitutes
And mourned with them the Bull of Heaven's death.

That night the wound Enkidu had received
In his struggle with Humbaba grew worse.
He tossed with fever and was filled with dreams.
He woke his friend to tell him what he heard and saw:
The gods have said that one of us must die
Because we killed Humbaba and the Bull of Heaven.
Enlil said I must die, for you are two-thirds god
And should not die. But Shamash spoke
For me and called me "innocent."
They all began to argue, as if that word
Touched off a universal rage.
I know that they have chosen me.
The tears flowed from his eyes.
My brother, it is the fever only,
Said Gilgamesh. Enkidu cursed the gate
Into Humbaba's forest that had lamed his hand

And cursed the hunter and the prostitute
Who had led him from his friends, not sensing
Gilgamesh's fear at the thought of his own solitude:
I can't imagine being left alone,
I'm less a man without my friend.
Gilgamesh did not let himself believe
The gods had chosen one of them to die.
The fever reached its height
And like a madman talking to a wall
In an asylum Enkidu cursed the gate
As if it were the person he could blame:
I would have split you with my ax
If I had known that you could wound.
Shamash, who called me "innocent," I curse
Your heart for bringing me to suffer this.
He thought he heard Shamash arguing
That if the prostitute had never come
To him he never would have known his friend
Who sat beside him now trying to find
The gesture to reverse the gods'
Decision or relieve
A close companion's pain.
Gilgamesh, though he was king,
Had never looked at death before.
Enkidu saw in him a helplessness
To understand or speak, as if this were
The thing the other had to learn
And he to teach. But visions from his sickness
Made him also helpless as a teacher.
All he had to give was being weak and rage
About the kings and elders and the animals
In the underworld that crowded sleep,
About the feathers that grew from his arms
In the house of dust whose occupants
Sat in the dark devoid of light
With clay as food, the fluttering of wings

47

As substitutes for life.
The priest and the ecstatic sat there too,
Their spirits gone, each body like an old recluse
No longer inhabiting its island.
Like shells one finds among shore rocks,
Only the slightest evidence
Of life survived.

Gilgamesh knew his friend was close to death.
He tried to recollect aloud their life together
That had been so brief, so empty of gestures
They never felt they had to make. Tears filled his eyes
As he appealed to Ninsun, his mother, and to the
    Elders
Not to explain but to save his friend
Who once had run among the animals,
The wild horses of the range, the panther of the Steppe.
He had run and drunk with them
. As if they were his brothers.
Just now he went with me into the forest of Humbaba
And killed the Bull of Heaven.

∽

Everything had life to me, he heard Enkidu murmur,
The sky, the storm, the earth, water, wandering,
The moon and its three children, salt, even my hand
Had life. It's gone. It's gone. I have seen death
As a total stranger sees another person's world,
Or as a freak sees whom the gods created
When they were drunk on too much wine
And had a contest to show off
The greatness of the harm that they could do,
Creating a man who had no balls or a woman
Without a womb, a crippled

Or deliberately maimed child
Or old age itself, blind eyes, trembling hands
Contorted in continual pain,
A starving dog too weak to eat,
A doe caught in a trap
Wincing for help,
Or death.
The contest rules the one who makes
The greatest wretchedness wins.
For all of these can never fit
Into the perfect state they made
When they were sober.
These are the things I have witnessed
As a man and weep for now
For they will have no witness if friends die.
I see them so alone and helpless,
Who will be kind to them?

He looked at Gilgamesh, and said:
You will be left alone, unable to understand
In a world where nothing lives anymore
As you thought it did.
Nothing like yourself, everything like dead
Clay before the river makes the plants
Burst out along its beds, dead and . . .
He became bitter in his tone again:
Because of *her*. She made me see
Things as a man, and a man sees death in things.
That is what it is to be a man. You'll know
When you have lost the strength to see
The way you once did. You'll be alone and wander
Looking for that life that's gone or some
Eternal life you have to find.
He drew closer to his friend's face.
My pain is that my eyes and ears

No longer see and hear the same
As yours do. Your eyes have changed.
You are crying. You never cried before.
It's not like you.
Why am I to die,
You to wander on alone?
Is that the way it is with friends?

Gilgamesh sat hushed as his friend's eyes stilled.
In his silence he reached out
To touch the friend whom he had lost.

III

Gilgamesh wept bitterly for his friend.
He felt himself now singled out for loss
Apart from everyone else. The word *Enkidu*
Roamed through every thought
Like a hungry animal through empty lairs
In search of food. The only nourishment
He knew was grief, endless in its hidden source
Yet never ending hunger.

All that is left to one who grieves
Is convalescence. No change of heart or spiritual
Conversion, for the heart has changed
And the soul has been converted
To a thing that sees
How much it costs to lose a friend it loved.

It has grown past conversion to a world
Few enter without tasting loss
In which one spends a long time waiting
For something to move one to proceed.
It is that inner atmosphere that has
An unfamiliar gravity or none at all
Where words are flung out in the air but stay
Motionless without an answer,
Hovering about one's lips
Or arguing back to haunt
The memory with what one failed to say,
Until one learns acceptance of the silence
Amidst the new debris
Or turns again to grief
As the only source of privacy,
Alone with someone loved.
It could go on for years and years,
And has, for centuries,
For being human holds a special grief
Of privacy within the universe
That yearns and waits to be retouched
By someone who can take away
The memory of death.

Gilgamesh wandered through the desert
Alone as he had never been alone
When he had craved but not known what he craved;
The dryness now was worse than the decay.
The bored know nothing of this agony
Waiting for diversion they have never lost.
Death had taken the direction he had gained.
He was no more a king
But just a man who now had lost his way
Yet had a greater passion to withdraw
Into a deeper isolation. Mad,

Perhaps insane, he tried
To bring Enkidu back to life
To end his bitterness,
His fear of death.
His life became a quest
To find the secret of eternal life
Which he might carry back to give his friend.

He had put on the skins of animals
And thrown himself in the dust, and now
He longed to hear the voice of one
Who still used words as revelations;
He yearned to talk to Utnapishtim,
The one who had survived the flood
And death itself, the one who knew the secret.

Before his loss, when he approached at night
The mountain passes where the lions slept
He raised his eyes to Sin, the moon god, and prayed.
Now he expected help from no one.
He tried to fall asleep despite the sounds
Of movement through the trees, his chest was tight
With needless fear Enkidu would have calmed.

When he arrived at the mountains of Mashu,
Whose peaks reach to the shores of Heaven
And whose roots descend to Hell, he saw
The Scorpion people who guard its gate,
Whose knowledge is awesome, but whose glance is
    death.

When he saw them, his face turned ashen with
    dismay,
But he bowed down to them, the only way to shield
    himself
Against effusions of their gaze.
The Scorpion man then recognized
In Gilgamesh the flesh of gods and told his wife:
This one is two-thirds god, one-third man
And can survive our view, then spoke to him:
Why have you come this route to us?
The way is arduous and long
And no one goes beyond.

I have come to see my father,*
Utnapishtim,
Who was allowed to go beyond.
I want to ask him about life and death,
To end my loss. My friend has died.
I want to bring him back to life.

The Scorpion interrupted him and laughed,
Being impatient with such tales and fearful of
    sentiment:
No one is able to explain, no one has gone
Beyond these mountains. There is only death.
There is no light beyond, just darkness
And cold and at daybreak a burning heat.
You will learn nothing that we do not know.
You will only come to grief.

I have been through grief! Gilgamesh screamed.
Even if there will be more of pain,

* Spiritual father, ancestor in the apotropaic sense.

And heat and cold, I will go on!
Open the gate to the mountains!

All right, go! the Scorpion man said,
As if in anger with a child
Who had not reached the age of reason.
The gate is open! His wife added:
Be careful of the darkness. Gilgamesh saw
His going frightened them. They only seemed secure.

He entered the Road of the Sun
Which was so shrouded in darkness
That he could see neither
What was ahead of him nor behind.
Thick was the darkness
And there was no light.
He could see neither
What was ahead nor behind.
For days he traveled in this blindness
Without a light to guide him,
Ascending or descending,
He could not be sure,
Going on with only
The companionship of grief
In which he felt Enkidu at his side.
He said his name: Enkidu, Enkidu,

To quiet his fear
Through the darkness
Where there was no light
And where he saw neither
What was ahead nor behind

Until before him
When it seemed there was no end
To loneliness
A valley came in view
Sprinkled with precious stones
And fruit-filled vines.

Gazing into the valley
He felt overcome with pain
As a man
Who has been in prison
Feels his chains
At his release from fear.
He spoke Enkidu's name aloud
As if explaining to the valley
Why he was there, wishing his friend
Could see the same horizon,
Share the same delights: My friend Enkidu
Died. We hunted together. We killed Humbaba
And the Bull of Heaven. We were always
At each other's side, encouraging when one
Was discouraged or afraid or didn't
Understand. He was this close to me.
He held his hands together to describe
The closeness. It seemed for a moment
He could almost touch his friend,

60

Could speak to him as if he were there:
Enkidu.   Enkidu.   But suddenly the silence
Was deeper than before
In a place where they had never been
Together.
He sat down on the ground and wept:
Enkidu.   Enkidu.

As when we can recall so vividly
We almost touch,
Or think of all the gestures that we failed
To make.

After several minutes he stood up
Explaining only to himself why he
Had come — To find the secret of eternal life
To bring Enkidu back to life —
Recognizing now the valley was deaf
To loss known only to himself.

This private mumbling made both time and distance
    pass
Until he reached the sea and came upon a cottage
Where a barmaid named Siduri lived. He beat the
    door
Impatiently. And when she called: Where are you
    going,
Traveler? and came to see, she saw him as
    half-crazed.
Perhaps he is a murderer! she thought
And drew away from him in fear.

Why do you draw back like that? he asked.
Has grief made me so terrible to look at?

Who are you? You are no one that I know.
I am Gilgamesh, who killed Humbaba
And the Bull of Heaven with my friend.

If you are Gilgamesh and did those things, why
Are you so emaciated and your face half-crazed?

I have grieved! Is it so impossible
To believe? he pleaded.
My friend who went through everything with me
Is dead!

No one grieves that much, she said.
Your friend is gone. Forget him.
No one remembers him. He is dead.

Enkidu.   Enkidu.   Gilgamesh called out:
Help me. They do not know you
As I know you.

Then she took pity on him
And let him enter and lie down and rest.
She gave him her bed to fall into and sleep
And rubbed his back and neck and legs and arms
When he was coming out of sleep, still muttering
About the one "who went with me through
     everything."
Like those old people who forget their listeners
Have not lived through their past with them,
Mentioning names that no one knows.
Enkidu, whom I loved so much,

Who went through everything with me.
He died — like any ordinary man.
I have cried both day and night.
I did not want to put him in a grave.
He will rise, I know, one day.
But then I saw that he *was* dead.
His face collapsed within
After several days,
Like cobwebs I have touched
With my finger.

She wiped his face with a moist cloth
Saying: Yes   yes   yes   yes,
As she made him cooler
Trying to help him to forget
By the steady softness of her flesh.
She moved her lips across his chest
And caressed the length of his tired body
And lay over him at night until he slept.

You will never find an end to grief by going on,
She said to the one half sleeping at her side,
Leaning forward to wipe the perspiration from his
    face.
His eyes were open though his whole self felt asleep
Far off alone in some deep forest
Planted in his flesh
Through which he felt his way in pain
Without the help
Of friends.
She spoke as to a child who could not understand
All the futility that lay ahead
Yet who she knew would go on to repeat

Repeat repeat the things men had to learn.
The gods gave death to man and kept life for
Themselves. That is the only way it is.
Cherish your rests; the children you might have;
You are a thing that carries so much tiredness.

When he arose, she washed his body and dressed him
And spoke of pleasures he could find with her
Instead of going on in foolishness.
But he, when he was fully awake,
Threw off the clothes she had put on
And dressed again in the dark pelts he had come so
    far in.

Her presence seemed to suffocate him now.
He wanted to throw off
Each pleasureful touch
And moment of forgetfulness

To bathe away

Her memory. To bathe
Was now more urgent
Than to sleep.
Tell me only the way
To Utnapishtim if you know.
Tell me the way to him,
I am going on!

No one has crossed the sea of death to him.
Will you? You are impetuous like all the rest.

Stay here and sleep. Begin your life again.
You have come so far. You need much sleep.

He was fully awake with desperate energy.
Tell me the way!

All right, she sighed;
She had despaired of him already.
You must find his boatman Urshanabi;
He has stone images that will show the way.
If it can be arranged for you, who are
So blind with love of self and with rage,
To reach the other side,
It will be through his help, his alone.
If it cannot be, then turn back.
I am still fool enough to take you in.
She turned in anger back to her house
And slammed the door, not listening
As he screamed at her: I am not blind
With self-love but with loss!
He felt his head split with the pain
Of making himself heard
By her, by all the world.
It was as if his mind exploded
Into little pieces. He struck at everything
In sight. He hurried with his ax
Drawn from his belt down to the shore
To find this Urshanabi.

Coming upon some stones that stood in his way
He smashed them into a thousand pieces.
Urshanabi, a lean old man with gray hair
Browned by the brackish water of his river,

Laughed at the stranger's folly and even
Danced to mock the crazed man's act.
You have destroyed the Sacred Stones
That might have taken you across!

Gilgamesh sat on the ground
His head resting on his drawn up knees,
Wondering how much fatigue
A man could stand.
He raised his head to speak:
I know I have broken them;
What difference now.
I only want to speak to Utnapishtim,
To reach his shore.
Can you help me?

Perhaps, the boatman said, but I have questions
To ask first. Why are your cheeks so thin?
Your eyes so full of grief?
What have you known of loss
That makes you different from other men?

Don't ask me to retell my pain, he said.
I only want to bring him back to life.

Whom? asked Urshanabi, and he laughed
At the presumption in this quest.

He was my friend, pleaded Gilgamesh,
Unconscious once again of audience and pain.
Recounting flowed from him

Like music played by someone else.
My younger brother who saved me from
The Bull of Heaven and Humbaba,
Who listened to my dreams,
Who shared my pain.
Why did he have to die?
He would have stayed with *me* in death.
He would not have let *me* die alone.
He was a friend.

He stopped, realizing
He had not come this far to hear himself
Recall the failure of his grief to save
But to find an end to his despair.

Which is the way to Utnapishtim? I must know!
Is it the sea? the mountains? I will go there!

I told you, Urshanabi said;
The stone images are destroyed.
If you had been as reverent with them
As with your friend, they might have helped you
    cross.

What else? What else is there?
There must be something else!

You are exhausting me, the boatman said.
I do not think that you will be serene

69

Ever, or at peace enough for others
Not to be exhausted by your presence
Until, at last, you lose by your own hand
The very thing you crave to hold alone.

Don't moralize at me! I have no love
For images, old gods, prophetic words.
I want to talk to Utnapishtim!
Tell me how.

Take your ax in your hand, said Urshanabi;
Go down into the forest, cut down
A boatload of long trees
And set them with bitumen.* They will be your poles
To push yourself across the sea of death.

When Gilgamesh heard this, he went to work.
And when the poles were cut and set with
Bitumen, the two men boarded Urshanabi's ship
And sailed the channel toward the sea of death.

❧

* Knobs of bitumen set at the upper end of each punting pole,
according to Babylonian custom. Cf. R. C. Thompson, ed., *The
Epic of Gilgamesh* (New York: Oxford University Press, 1930),
p. 85.

Now Gilgamesh was alone. The boatman's voice
Could still be heard, but faintly, from the shore.
Don't let the waters touch your hand.
Take a second pole, a third, a fourth
When each is rotted by the sea of death.

When he had used each pole but one
He pulled his clothes off his body
And with this last remaining pole
He made a mast, his clothes as sail,
And drifted on the sea of death.

∽

Utnapishtim stood on the other shore,
His old and rugged features worn
By the seas and deserts he himself had crossed.
He wondered why the Sacred Stones had been
    destroyed,
Why the boat was only drifting.
And who the man was
Who resembled loss itself.
Before the ship had touched his shore he thought,
I am afraid that nothing here can help him.

The eyes of Utnapishtim seemed so full
Of hospitality
When Gilgamesh awoke

From his exhaustion.
As if some faces could be doorways in-
To life one has an image of
But never sees. The vista was
A strange and beautiful
Release.
Utnapishtim was the only one whom he had met
On his journey who did not add to
His fatigue.
Gilgamesh was speaking but only to relieve
His weight of grief,
Not to demand an understanding:
My friend has died so many times in me,
And yet he still seems so alive,
Like a younger brother,
Then suddenly like soft tissue,
A dried leaf.
I was afraid.
Is there something more than death?
Some other end to friendship?
I came to you whom they call "The Distant,"
I crossed the mountains and the sea.
I was like a blind man, but not one
From whom someone in search can draw light.
I am so tired, so tired. I have
Killed bear, hyena, stag, ibex for food
And clothes. I barely crossed the sea of death.

Utnapishtim raised his hand and touched the shoulder
Of the younger man to put him at his ease.
Two things encourage me to hope, he said;
That one can come this far to bring life to a friend
And that you understand how we must borrow light
From the blind. (My own right eye was damaged
    long ago

And my left is slowly decaying.)
Friendship is vowing toward immortality
And does not know the passing away of beauty
(Though take care!)
Because it aims for the spirit.
Many years ago through loss I learned
That love is wrung from our inmost heart
Until only the loved one is and we are not.
You have known, O Gilgamesh,
What interests me,
To drink from the Well of Immortality.
Which means to make the dead
Rise from their graves
And the prisoners from their cells,
The sinners from their sins.
I think love's kiss kills our heart of flesh.
It is the only way to eternal life,
Which should be unbearable if lived
Among the dying flowers
And the shrieking farewells
Of the overstretched arms of our spoiled hopes.

I think compassion is our God's pure act
Which burns forever,
And be it in Heaven or in Hell
Doesn't matter for me; because
Hell is the everlasting gift
Of His presence
To the lonely heart who is longing
Amidst perishing phantoms and doesn't care
To find any immortality
If not in the pure loneliness of the Holy One,
This loneliness which He enjoys forever
Inside and outside of His creation.
It is enough for one who loves

To find his Only One singled in Himself.
And that is the cup of immortality!

Gilgamesh looked into the face of the older man
In whom he saw this loneliness.
He could still feel the touch of Utnapishtim's hand.

Time and space were uneventful now.
Nothing inclined him to impatience.
They talked together, walked
And sat on rocks.
The older man seemed pleased
To have his company
As if an absent son or other loss
Had been slightly returned to him.
In time the younger felt
He knew him well enough
To say:
You sometimes seem to have a downcast look
As if the life you have found here still
Has failed to bring you peace.
How did you come to find this world
And reach this life?

I did not come out of desire like you,
Said Utnapishtim; I was the choice of others.
They walked along the shore
And the older man told his story.

There was a city called Shurrupak
On the bank of the Euphrates.
It was very old and so many were the gods
Within it. They converged in their complex hearts
On the idea of creating a great flood.
There was Anu, their aging and weak-minded father,
The military Enlil, his adviser,
Ishtar, the sensation craving one,
And all the rest. Ea, who was present
At their council, came to my house
And, frightened by the violent winds that filled the
     air,
Echoed all that they were planning and had said.
Man of Shurrupak, he said, tear down your house

And build a ship. Abandon your possessions
And the works that you find beautiful and crave
And save your life instead. Into the ship
Bring the seed of all the living creatures.

I was overawed, perplexed,
And finally downcast. I agreed to do
As Ea said but I protested: What shall I say
To the city, the people, the leaders?

Tell them, Ea said, you have learned that Enlil
The war god despises you and will not
Give you access to the city anymore.
Tell them for this Ea will bring the rains.

That is the way gods think, he laughed. His tone
Of savage irony frightened Gilgamesh
Yet gave him pleasure, being his friend.
They only know how to compete or echo.

But who am I to talk? He sighed as if
Disgusted with himself; I did as he
Commanded me to do. I spoke to them
And some came out to help me build the ship
Of seven stories each with nine chambers.
The boat was cube in shape, and sound; it held
The food and wine and precious minerals
And seed of living animals we put
In it. My family then moved inside
And all who wanted to be with us there:
The game of the field, the goats of the Steppe,
The craftsmen of the city came, a navigator

Came. And then Ea ordered me to close
The door. The time of the great rains had come.
O there was ample warning, yes, my friend,
But it was terrifying still. Buildings
Blown by the winds for miles like desert brush.
People clung to branches of trees until
Roots gave way. New possessions, now debris,
Floated on the water with their special
Sterile vacancy. The riverbanks failed
To hold the water back. Even the gods
Cowered like dogs at what they had done.
Ishtar cried out like a woman at the height
Of labor: O how could I have wanted
To do this to my people! They were *hers*,
Notice. Even her sorrow was possessive.
Her spawn that she had killed too soon.
Old gods are terrible to look at when
They weep, all bloated like spoiled fish.
One wonders if they ever understand
That they have caused their grief. When the seventh
   day
Came, the flood subsided from its slaughter
Like hair drawn slowly back
From a tormented face.
I looked at the earth and all was silence.
Bodies lay like alewives dead
And in the clay. I fell down
On the ship's deck and wept. Why? Why did they
Have to die! I couldn't understand. I asked
Unanswerable questions a child asks
When a parent dies — for nothing. Only slowly
Did I make myself believe — or hope — they
Might all be swept up in their fragments
Together
And made whole again
By some compassionate hand.

But my hand was too small
To do the gathering.
I have only known this feeling since
When I look out across the sea of death,
This pull inside against a littleness — myself —
Waiting for an upward gesture.

O the dove, the swallow and the raven
Found their land. The people left the ship.
But I for a long time could only stay inside.
I could not face the deaths I knew were there.
Then I received Enlil, for Ea had *chosen* me;
The war god touched my forehead; he blessed
My family and said:
Before this you were just a man, but now
You and your wife shall be like gods. You
Shall live in the distance at the rivers' mouth,
At the source. I allowed myself to be
Taken far away from all that I had seen.
Sometimes even in love we yearn to leave mankind.
Only the loneliness of the Only One
Who never acts like gods
Is bearable.
I am downcast because of what I've seen,
Not what I still have hope to yearn for.
Lost youths restored to life,
Lost children to their crying mothers,
Lost wives, lost friends, lost hopes, lost homes,
I want to bring these back to them.
But now there is you.
We must find something for you.
How will you find eternal life
To bring back to your friend?

He pondered busily, as if
It were just a matter of getting down to work
Or making plans for an excursion.
Then he relaxed, as if there were no use
In this reflection. I would grieve
At all that may befall you still
If I did not know you must return
And bury your own loss and build
Your world anew with your own hands.
I envy you your freedom.

As he listened, Gilgamesh felt tiredness again
Come over him, the words now so discouraging,
The promise so remote, so unlike what he sought.
He looked into the old man's face, and it seemed
    changed,
As if this one had fought within himself a battle
He would never know, that still went on.

They returned to Utnapishtim's house
And to his aged wife who seemed to Gilgamesh
In her shufflings and her faithful silence
Like a servant only there to hold the door.
He hardly knew her as a person,
He had talked only to Utnapishtim,
Been only with him.
Was she all he needed as companion?

Yet when he fell asleep and Utnapishtim
Remarked to his wife with hostile irony:
Look at the strong man who wants life;
Sleep follows him like his shadow,

She said to her husband:
Touch him again and wake him
So he can return in peace to his home.
She had learned to read her husband's moods.

Men are deceitful and incapable of peace.
I know! He said. Can't he even stay awake with me?
Sleep is like death only slothful people yearn for.
Bake loaves, he ordered her, and put them at his head
One for each day he sleeps.
We'll see how long it is before he wakes.

Over her frail protest the trial was set.
After some days, Utnapishtim woke the younger man
Who thought he had barely gone to sleep.

You have slept for seven days, he said.
Look at the dried out loaves my wife has baked.
How will you bear eternal life?
It is not easy to live like gods.

What can I do to win eternal life?
The younger pleaded.
Wherever I go — even here — I am drawn back
To death.

Austerely Utnapishtim called out to the boatman
On the other shore and scolded him
For sending Gilgamesh across.
Return him to your shore, he called.

Bathe him and burn these pelts he wears
Which can only remind him of his friend.
Let him be fresh and young again.
Let the band around his head be changed.
Let him return to his city untired.
His people need the sight of something new,
And the appearance of success.
His words sounded bitter.

I came for wisdom only, shouted Gilgamesh.

Don't hurt an old man further with your praise.
I have nothing to give you that will save.

Urshanabi crossed in his ship and obeyed.
He took the pelts from Gilgamesh,
And though the grieving man
Was too disheartened to protest,
When they were taken from him and burned
He cried out as if a festered wound had just
Been pierced. When it was over
He stood in the bow to leave
With only inner traces of his journey.
Utnapishtim contemplated him, unable to speak.
As if he were afraid of some desire to retain,
He looked down at the ground, away from
    Gilgamesh.

His wife whispered to him, saying:
He has come so far.
Have you forgotten how grief fastened onto you
And made you crave some word, some gesture, once?

Utnapishtim's face grew tight, then relaxed,
As when one is relieved of inner pain
By one who sees more deeply than oneself.
He looked at the younger man
Who had come into his consciousness. Youth is very
Cruel to an old face,
He said in a hushed voice.
It looks into its lines for wisdom
So touchingly
But there is nothing there to find.

Gilgamesh wanted to reach out to tell him
He was wrong, sensing suddenly the hours
One might spend alone in contemplating oldness
As he himself had spent alone in his spoiled youth,
Seeing nothing there but time.

I know your pain too well to lie,
Said Utnapishtim.
I will tell you a secret I have never told.
Something to take back with you and guard.
There is a plant in the river. Its thorns
Will prick your hands as a rose thorn pricks
But it will give to you new life.

He heard these words and tried to speak
But rushed instead to the old man and embraced him.
The two men held each other for a moment
Then Utnapishtim raised his hands
As if to say: Enough.
And Gilgamesh looked back at him
Then hurried off to find the plant.

84

He tied stones to his feet and descended
Into the river. When he saw the plant
Of rich rose color and ambrosial
Shimmering in the water like a prism
Of the sunlight, he seized it, and it cut
Into his palms. He saw his blood flow in the water.

He cut the stones loose from his feet and rose
Up sharply to the surface and swam to shore.
He was calling out, I have it! I have it!

Urshanabi guided the ecstatic man away
To the other shore, and when they parted
Gilgamesh was alone again, but not
With loneliness or the memory of death.
He stopped to drink and rest beside a pool
And soon undressed and let himself slip in
The water quietly until he was refreshed,
Leaving the plant unguarded on the ground.

A serpent had smelled its sweet fragrance and saw
Its chance to come from the water, and devoured
The plant, shedding its skin as slough.

When Gilgamesh rose from the pool,

His naked body glistening and refreshed,
The plant was gone; the discarded skin
Of a serpent was all he saw. He sat
Down on the ground, and wept.

IV

In time he recognized this loss
As the end of his journey
And returned to Uruk.

Perhaps, he feared,
His people would not share
The sorrow that he knew.

He entered the city and asked a blind man
If he had ever heard the name Enkidu,
And the old man shrugged and shook his head,
Then turned away,
As if to say it is impossible

To keep the names of friends
Whom we have lost.

Gilgamesh said nothing more
To force his sorrow on another.

He looked at the walls,
Awed at the heights
His people had achieved
And for a moment — just a moment —
All that lay behind him
Passed from view.

Names and Places
Appearing in the Narrative

About the *Gilgamesh*

An Autobiographical
Postscript

Names and Places
Appearing in the Narrative

Anu (A'nu): The father of the Sumerian gods. The cosmic mountain, created from the primeval sea, had two parts: heaven (An) and earth (Ki), divided by the god Enlil, who proceeded to manage the affairs of the latter, with Anu overseeing the former. A temple in Uruk bore his name

Bull of Heaven: Figure of drought created by Anu for Ishtar as a punisment for Gilgamesh's arrogance

Ea (E'a): God of fresh springs; patron of the arts; friend of mankind

Enkidu (En-ki'du): Friend of Gilgamesh; figure of natural man; patron saint of animals. A goddess of creation, Aruru, was supposed to have created him on the Steppe from clay in the image of Anu

Enlil (En'lil): God of earth, wind, and spirit. He is merged in the present narrative with Ninurta, the war god

Gilgamesh (Gil'ga-mesh): Fifth king of Uruk after the great flood; son of the goddess-prophetess Ninsun and of a priest of Uruk. He is two-thirds god, one-third man, noted as a builder-king

Humbaba (Hum-ba'ba): Guardian of the cedar forest; nature divinity; killed by Gilgamesh and Enkidu

Ishtar (Ish'tar): Goddess of love and fertility, and of war; the daughter of Anu; patroness of Uruk

Ishullanu (I'shul-la'nu): Anu's gardener; rejected by Ishtar, who turned him into a mole

Mashu (Ma'shu): A mountain with twin peaks (the Lebanon ranges), behind which the sun descends at nightfall and out of which it rises at dawn

Ninsun (Nin'sun): Mother of Gilgamesh; minor goddess known for wisdom

Scorpion man and woman: Guardians of the entrance to Mashu

Shamash (Sha'mash): The sun; husband and brother of Ishtar; son of Sin, the moon god

Siduri (Sid-ur'i): Classic barmaid who lives by the sea

Urshanabi (Ur'sha-na'bi): The boatman of Utnapishtim at the waters of the dead. His actual role in the epic, a subject of numerous scholarly studies and interpretations, is greatly reduced in this narrative

Uruk (Ur'uk): Biblical Erech in southern Babylonia; seat of an important dynasty of kings following the flood

Utnapishtim (Ut'na-pish'tim): Wise man of Shurrupak, one of the oldest cities of Mesopotamia, situated about twenty miles north of Uruk. His name means "He who saw life." He was protected from the flood by Ea

About the *Gilgamesh*

In the nineteneth century a number of clay tablets on which the *Gilgamesh* was written were discovered in the temple library and palace ruins in Nineveh, once the capital of the ancient Assyrian empire, by two Englishmen, Austen H. Layard and George Smith, both of the British Museum, and the Turkish archaeologist Hormuzd Rassam. In 1872 George Smith delivered a paper before the Society of Biblical Archaeology which included his partial translation of the cuneiform texts along with an analysis of several episodes of the *Gilgamesh* epic, especially the narrative of the flood. The reaction to this "new" material, with its far-reaching implications for Biblical history in particular, was one of great enthusiasm and curiosity, and spurred others on to further explorations in the ruins of Mesopotamia's ancient cities and to an expanded study of cuneiform inscriptions in general.

This spreading interest and scholarly research led to the discovery of other tablets and fragments concerning Gilgamesh and his adventures, and, eventually, to a continuing appearance of annotated editions and translations in European languages which, if not yet definitive, have been based on steadily accumulated knowledge.

The epic, in at least a number of its stories, was Sumerian in origin and was later added to and unified as a national epic by the Semitic Babylonians, heirs in the Tigris and Euphrates valley to Sumerian culture and civilization. The tablets from Nineveh, which constitute the largest extant portion of the epic, date from the seventh century B.C. and were probably collected at that time from much older Sumerian texts and translated into the contemporary Akkadian Semitic language at the request of King Assur-bani-pal for his palace library. From the existence of tablets found elsewhere in Mesopotamia and in parts of Anatolia in the older Sumerian language and in Hurrian and Hittite translations, each depicting portions of the *Gilgamesh* story, scholars have been able to date the epic at about 2000 B.C. However, the most recent scholarship believes that all extant portions are copies of still older originals deriving from a much earlier time, and moves the epic's creation back as far as the third millennium B.C. It is virtually impossible to determine when the material was first written down, let alone when it originated orally or how long it existed in an oral tradition. Rather it can be assumed, from the materials handed down from succeeding ancient peoples and languages, that it was not composed all of a piece and at one time but was added to gradually and varied by many tellers.

The *Gilgamesh* is unquestionably older than either the Bible or the Homeric epics; it predates the latter by at least a millennium and a half. The discovery of a fragment of the epic in Palestine suggests the existence of a version known to early Biblical authors. Though we cannot know how widespread knowledge of the *Gilgamesh* epic was in the ancient Near East, we can say with surety that it is one of man's oldest and most enduring stories.

As to Gilgamesh's historical identity, the Sumerian king list establishes a Gilgamesh as fifth in line of the First Dynasty of kingship of Uruk following the great flood recorded in the epic, placing him approximately in the latter half of the third millennium. He was supposed to have reigned a hundred and twenty-six years. He was known as the builder of the wall of Uruk, and his mother was said to be the goddess Ninsun, wife of a god named Lugalbanda, who however was not his father. His real father was, according to the king list, a high priest of Kullab, a district of Uruk, from whom he derived his mortality. These few details are drawn from the epic itself and from a number of Sumerian inscriptions listing kings, rulers, and princes. Gilgamesh's name was associated with many stories and fabulous adventures as well as with the experience of grief.

Probably there was a Gilgamesh and he was endowed by tradition with a superhuman mind and spirit. Perhaps if we were to doubt the reality of Gilgamesh because of the folkloric hyperbole about him and his emotions as drawn in the epic, we would have to doubt whatever it is in ourselves that identifies with him — or, for that matter, with the Biblical Job or the Shakespearean King Lear. Looked at in this light, the *Gilgamesh* has survived in our world because a constellation of our emotions is reflected in it. We could almost say that anything so profoundly human as the image of Gilgamesh was bound to reappear, yet we are still surprised to learn that one of the very oldest stories of man is so inherently contemporary.

It is the epic's emotional power which assures its place in world literature. The *Gilgamesh* is a kind of touchstone to other, more "modern" works. It reminds us of many stories of the Bible and episodes in Homer that are part of our cultural consciousness: of the universality of the friendship theme and of the experience of heartbreak over loss, of Achilles' reaction to the death of his friend Patroklos in the *Iliad*, or even the depth of Lear's grief at his daughter Cordelia's death.

Certain structural formulas in the *Gilgamesh*, of recurring themes and architecturally sequential episodes (which in this instance scholars have had to reconstruct tentatively), places it in the company of the *Odyssey* and the *Iliad*. Though non-oral epics like Virgil's *Aeneid* and Dante's *Divine Comedy* have an intellectual coherence to us which it lacks, its intense and sophisticated grouping of stories around the theme of death and the human challenge to death gives it an elemental coherence which cements and heightens its otherwise rambling structure, and places it in their magnificent company.

What such "classics" do for us by the very rarity of their occurrence is to give us what W. H. Auden once called "a high holiday." They show us, by their concentration on a great soul's struggles to reach a passionately desired goal, our essential human drama raised beyond our everyday recurring life. They show rather than preach how acceptance of limitations in the face of metaphysical facts actually occurs. They begin in a world where impending doom is felt as a living force and gain their momentum as the individual feels power to challenge that force and finally to obtain the spiritual courage to accept the danger of being crushed by its superior power and mystery. In the *Gilgamesh*, particularly, life is very serious and "the world is redundant with life," as Thorkild Jacobsen says in *Before Philosophy*. This seriousness is expressed in the total oneness of people, animals, plants, dreams, and what to us would seem dead things, stones and gates. Professor Jacobsen has described the inner action of the *Gilgamesh* as "a revolt against death." This revolt, in a universe once thought to be ordered and good, grows from a belief that death is evil and a crime against humanity's growing consciousness of human rights. Hence, it is an outcry on behalf of life and its injured kindredness.

The survival of this great poem in the world must relate partly to the survival of the same vision in a few people in our world, people who may not consciously believe in personified gods nor have culturally handed-down names to give them, but who through pain of loss may have made this "revolt," or through compassion may understand how intimately related they really are to all the creatures and things of the universe. In an age in which we consume and are consumed by a superfluity of one-dimensional images, this poem calls us to be profound. And in a war age in which all kindredness is overlooked and life and substance are destroyed indiscriminately, this very old story reminds us what human history, our destiny, and we ourselves really are.

At the end of the epic a serpent finds the power to renew its life, which a man had sought and finally lost. In a very large sense, the reader must decide what that ending means for himself. It is an inward problem. One can view the loss tragically, as perhaps the Sumerians and Babylonians did, and despair in this as the ultimate fate of man. Or one can believe and hope that for the human being the experience of wisdom is more important than possession of even the highest things.

There are extant tablets which can be viewed as sequels to this ending. One depicts the death and regal funeral of an old and honored Gilgamesh. Another contains a Semitic version of part of a Sumerian story relating additional experiences of Gilgamesh and Enkidu.* This tablet tells of a sacred tree which Gilgamesh has lost to the Underworld. Enkidu, the one who brings back lost things, offers to go down into the Underworld and retrieve it for his friend. The story includes a long lamentation by Gilgamesh over the loss of the tree and an illusion of Enkidu's physical return after death has devoured him in the Underworld. From this latter illusion the tablet has been called "Enkidu's Resurrection."

These and other stories about Gilgamesh have not been included in the present narrative for reasons of dramatic unity.

The following lines are based on the last portion of Gilgamesh and Enkidu's illusory reunion and, as

* See Alexander Heidel, *The Gilgamesh Epic and Old Testament Parallels*, 2d ed. (Chicago, 1949) and Samuel N. Kramer, *Sumerian Mythology* (Philadelphia, 1944).

an interpretation only, represent an afterglimpse into
Gilgamesh's state of grief.

One night in his loneliness
Gilgamesh pleaded with Ea
To open the door of death
To let the spirit of Enkidu
Return to him a moment.

For a moment, by Ea's grace,
The two friends met
And almost touched. Gilgamesh
Could not hold back his tears
And begged him to come near.

You have wept enough for me,
Enkidu said.
A friend is not allowed to add to grief.
I have grown weak, devoured
In my flesh. You must not try to touch me.

I need to see you are the same,
Cried Gilgamesh.

I am afraid that you will hate
The friendship we have known
Because it did not last forever.

Gilgamesh, not listening, reached out
To the image of his friend
Trying to see what Ea veiled.

If you are my friend, Enkidu said,
You must not touch me. Treat me
As Utnapishtim treated you.

He gave me a plant
He knew that I would lose!
He gave you the wisdom of your soul.

Gilgamesh stood still
In the darkness, conscious
Of the silence once again
And of the shadows which had held for years
The absence of his friend,
As if just drawn
From recollection
Back to life.

The noises in his city
And laughter from outside
Had reached his ears, or was
It just another dream
Or Ea's further tricks of grace?

No matter which, he went outside
To see himself
Just what had drawn them
Into celebration.

    Since the discoveries of the *Gilgamesh* episodes and
the subsequent efforts to assemble them into an or-
ganic and logically sequential whole, numerous scholarly translations based directly on the cuneiform
texts have been made into modern languages.

Most important among those consulted for the present narrative, which represents a personal attempt to revivify the *Gilgamesh* in a free form as a living poem, are Alexander Heidel's *The Gilgamesh Epic and Old Testament Parallels,* 2d ed. (Chicago, 1949); E. A. Speiser's translation in James B. Pritchard's *Ancient Near Eastern Texts,* 2d ed. (Princeton, 1955); R. Campbell Thompson, *The Epic of Gilgamesh* (London, 1928; textual edition, Oxford, 1930); Erich Ebeling in Gressmann's *Altorientalische Texte zum Alten Testament* (Berlin and Leipzig, 1926); and G. Contenau, *L'Épopeé de Gilgamesh* (Paris, 1939).

The basic work of S. N. Kramer has been consulted extensively, particularly his brilliant study *Sumerian Mythology* (Philadelphia, 1944; revised edition, New York, 1961). His "Sumerian Literature, a General Survey," in G. Ernest Wright's *The Bible and the Ancient Near East, Essays in Honor of William Foxwell Albright* (New York, 1961), pp. 249–266, is to be recommended as an excellent survey of the extant work and genres of Sumerian literature.

I am indebted to the thought and work of Thorkild Jacobsen, particularly to his essay "Mesopotamia," available in Henri Frankfort's *Before Philosophy* (Chicago, 1946), for the pictures he gives of deities, institutions, and human attitudes in the Mesopotamia of Gilgamesh's time.

An Autobiographical
Postscript

The *Gilgamesh* story first came to my attention in 1954 when I was a junior at Harvard taking a course in Oral Epic Tradition given by Dr. Albert Lord. Lord, a student of the late Milman Parry, had followed his very original teacher in pursuing the sources of oral tradition through its surviving practitioners among the Yugoslav epic folk singers. He had constructed at Harvard a sound theory and a sound course on epic transmission and form, working back from recordings of living Yugoslav epics, which permitted close analysis of theme and structural repetition, to Anglo-Saxon, Germanic, Scandinavian, Russian, the Greek epics of Homer and his contemporaries, the Iranian and the ancient Near Eastern creation epics, and the *Epic of Gilgamesh.* We did not work chronologically, but rather from the more primitive to the more sophisticated forms, *sophisticated* being a term Lord applied especially to the *Gilgamesh* epic because of its central emphasis on the human experience (which German scholars call "the becoming human") of the hero and the peripheral emphasis on the gods.

I had never heard of this epic before and, though I had read both major Homeric poems previously, as well as the non-oral epics of Virgil, Dante, Milton and, if *Faust* qualifies, Goethe, I had only the slightest knowlèdge of the epic experience, structure, and dimension, and even less knowledge of the more strictly oral and the more primitive forms.

When I read E. A. Speiser's translation of *Gilgamesh,* I felt a very special affinity with this epic. I knew it on a psychological and spiritual level. I lost interest in the other epics, stopped going to Dr. Lord's fine lectures, not because they lacked interest for me, but because I was audaciously secluding myself in an empty room in Emerson Hall writing an "Epic of Gilgamesh" in longhand and in *my* style, saying what I had (and needed) to say.

Of course, solitude without spiritual guidance can be very perilous; mine was academically disastrous as well as literarily futile, except for the fact that Gilgamesh entered my consciousness and my memory deeply and even methodically through this failure. His experience became a headlight to my own, and this headlight had its way of leading me to other persons, here and abroad, who had been similarly secluded.

In Cambridge the widow of Henry Ware Eliot, T. S. Eliot's brother, showed me her husband's research and her remarkable line drawings of Mesopotamian seals and artifacts of Gilgamesh's time, which they had worked on together following his retirement from business. A solitary scholar in Paris, Madeleine David, showed me her published interpretations of Gilgamesh, which followed closely those of certain German scholars who tended to identify Gilgamesh's exploits with those of Siegfried, an interpretation I tended to shy from. Albert Lord had held the notion that Gilgamesh, rather than being a superhero with only one minor flaw, was a kind of antihero whose only heroism consisted in his continuing his journey, not from any feat of strength, godlike invulnerability, moral foresight or circumspection, or spiritual wisdom within himself.

Further, my vision of Gilgamesh was influenced by English literary traditions of naturalism, tragic irony, and compassion. I also met a scholar at the Institut Catholique in Paris, Père Henri Cazelles, who retold the *Epic of Gilgamesh* as his first lecture each year to his biblical students and seminarians. I sat with him one day in the solitude of his second-floor study in that old institution, realizing his seclusion resembled my own, though, indeed, he had found his outlet. It is, after all, a story that is understood immediately by anyone who has suffered loss, a loss one has yearned to restore and finally has had to accept.

When I first read the epic I felt I had received a wound, or rather, I felt that a wound in me had been exposed. My own father had died when I was seven. This had been a very shattering loss for me, and I did not really free myself from my preoccupation with death until I was in my teens.

The wound was reopened deeply when I reached Harvard, by two events of that third year. The first was the discovery of *Gilgamesh*, the second was the discovery that a very close friend, a young man a little older than I, had Hodgkin's disease of which he was to die within two years.

Jack Kotteman was a Teaching Fellow in English at Harvard, a splendid mimic, a memorizer and reciter of English poetry's greatest and worst lines, an enthusiastic wanderer-companion when he had his energy and a very melancholy thinning figure when he did not. The last two years of life for him were wasting ones which he spent in and out of the Boston hospitals undergoing debilitating tests and transfusions and during which he tried to gain some strength from friends. There were those who were closer to him than I — especially his roommate, now Professor David Hart of Arkansas University, and the novelist Ilona Karmel, who was with him just before he died — but he reopened fully for me my particular sense of gratuitous loss and led me once again into solitude from my own helplessness in the face of death.

Deaths due to war or other acts involving human morality in some discernible way must be opposed and to some extent can be and are; but a death which has no apparent relation to morality leaves the survivor, if he loved the one who died, helpless and half-crazed, trying to explain, understand, protest, reverse the gratuitous, or reenter the real world with some trace of the old normalcy that has been lost. To be sure, the lonely frustration of the survivors is the same after every death, immorally or otherwise caused. And everyone is wise in saying, There is nothing you can do; but such wisdom does not reconcile any of us really to loss, for we knew the other as a person in himself not as an abstraction we could do without. We lost the one who we didn't realize enabled us to live in other people's worlds; now we have only our own private world and the almost herculean task of constructing a human reentry. What we finally do, out of desperation to recover the sense of the "outside," is to go on an impossible, or even forbidden, journey or pilgrimage, which from a rational point of view is futile: to find the one wise man, whomever or wherever he may be (and we all have it engrained in our metaphysical consciousness, no matter in what age we live, that such a wise man exists or should exist as witness to Wisdom); and to find from him the secret of eternal life or the secret of adjusting to this life as best we can.

Though not versed exactly in such Gilgameshian terms then, that was the motive in my going abroad back in the mid-1950s. I simply had to break out of my self-enclosure of loss to find a way to translate my experience into wisdom. As belief is born from desire, I believed in Wisdom. Two friends in Paris helped me to understand two essential ingredients of Wisdom, the third ingredient being acceptance, referred to before, which one can only come by within oneself on one's return.

The first of these friends was an Orientalist of the Collège de France, Louis Massignon. Massignon was well known in France, not only among scholars, writers, and other intellectuals, but also among ordinary newspaper readers who found his name associated with nonviolent street demonstrations against the Algerian war. He was especially known among Muslims, to whom his home was a virtual sanctuary.

By many in the field of Oriental studies he was regarded as the most original and, if you will, "selfless" Western student of Islam of the twentieth century. Many other celebrated Orientalists of his time have on occasion been unable to conceal either their admiration for or their jealousy of him. He was decidedly controversial all his life. And at his death not a few regarded him as a saint or a genius or a foolish old man. Outside the fields of Oriental studies, comparative religion, religious psychology, and sociology (the latter being the field in which he held his chair at the Collège), he is still known only relatively well, especially in the United States, though he did lecture at Chicago and Harvard universities. His name is often linked with those of Gandhi, Maritain, Claudel, Valéry, Teilhard de Chardin, Huysmans, Charles de Foucauld, or Jung, all of whom were his personal friends; and members of scientific academies in Moscow, Cairo, London, Delhi, and Tokyo still recall anecdotes about him at conferences. No one who met him has forgotten him, as if he were still alive and the encounter is now. He wrote me once, in 1959, from his summer home in Brittany:

51 years ago I built my new life of Faith in urging our Lord to take out of death (of sin) the friend who had led me (indirectly) through his sin to eternal love: teaching me in a crooked way that Love was to surrender, to be wrung from our inmost heart, so as to have only in mind His will, not mine.

Just before he died at seventy-nine in 1962, he asked his colleague Louis Gardet to be sure that as many people as possible came to know about Hallaj — the great Muslim mystic executed by caliphal court edict in Baghdad in 922 A.D. for "heresy" (as Massignon used to say, "crucified for love") — the study of whom had been his lifework. It was typical of Louis Massignon that on his deathbed he would ask someone nearby to pass on the knowledge of someone other than himself. Wisdom from him was a life given selflessly in hospitality to others.

The other friend was the Italian painter Dino Cavallarri. I met Dino in 1959 when I happened by chance onto an exhibition of his paintings and illustrations in the little Salon du Thé gallery on the Ile de la Cité in Paris. I was sufficiently impressed by his work to seek out his whereabouts and go to his studio to see more of it. When I returned to the United States a year later, I brought several of his paintings with me.

We kept in close touch; I learned of his successes in one-man shows in Paris and of his work in theater designs and book illustration. In January 1967, on my way to Istanbul, I stopped for a few days and spent my evenings with him and his family. He showed me his splendid illustrations for a new French edition of *Don Quixote,* and one evening I recounted for him in French the *Gilgamesh* epic, of which he had never heard. I told him he might try to pick up Contenau's translation. In May of that year he sent me, without any forewarning, three packages of color illustrations of the *Gilgamesh* story. He said they had given him more pleasure than any other illustrations he had made; I hope that one day they may appear in an exhibition all their own. I was deeply touched by his fraternity. I hadn't realized it, but it was so, that I never would have been able to extract Gilgamesh from my seclusion without the vision, the illustration, of a friend.

Massignon, with whom I talked many times about *Gilgamesh,* said to me once that it was enough for one who knew loss to have given love. "You must decide the end. You must finish *your Gilgamesh.*"

My ambitions are considerably less at thirty-eight than they were at twenty-two, or, at least my presumptions are less. I have worked in academic life sufficiently long to be cautious and skeptical as well as patient, and I have familiarized myself with my solitude repeatedly enough to know the limitations of my gifts for extracting something that must have been, in its ancient form, of transcendent beauty. I have also learned from lecturing on *Gilgamesh* that oral presentation is more moving than printed narrative, for the audience helps draw out and enlarge the work from the one who has been secluded with it. I know why Henri Cazelles delivered, rather than assigned as "outside reading," *his Gilgamesh.*

The present verse narrative, made only after years of inward companionship and meditation, of trying to forget and of being unable to forget, and based on literal scholarly translations, is intended as a subjective evocation that may bring the story and its principal characters more intimately to others than literal translations can do. I have not tried to "write an epic," as we have come to define it, which would be impossible for my non-Miltonic gifts. I have tried to retell an old story simply and to infuse it with as much passion, immediacy, and specific wisdom as I have known. At times my line of narration is very prosy indeed, at times I hope I achieve poetry in the evocation.

My cavalier view of the gods will arouse criticism among scholars of the ancient Near East, but it is one I suspect they themselves share and, I hope, will be forgiven if the overall evocation of the life and mood conveys the spirit of the anceint story itself. The monotheism of Utnapishtim in this narration will have

114

to be accepted by these scholars as part of any modern retelling, though some may even argue that it had its roots in the original.

Finally, I wish to mention the name of John Anson Kittredge. John was a young writer who died prematurely and in whose name his parents established a memorial scholarship for young writers and scholars. On the recommendation of my friend Walter Muir Whitehill, director of the Boston Athenaeum Library, I was awarded the first of these scholarships, back in 1957, to help support my work on *Gilgamesh.*

All told it has been fifteen years since I began working on "my *Gilgamesh,*" with time out for other writing, teaching, and a doctorate in Near Eastern Languages and Literatures at Harvard. Now I am only sorry that the Kittredges themselves, before their deaths, did not receive this expression from me of my gratitude for their gift in memory of their only son. This narrative is, in one important sense, for those who have known loss.

Gilgamesh: An Afterword
by John H. Marks

The most renowned of ancient Near Eastern
heroes is Gilgamesh, who has been dubbed "the
hero par excellence of the ancient world" and "the
hero without peer of the entire ancient Near East."[1]
This heroic figure has been known to the world
since George Smith introduced the first fragments
of the *Gilgamesh Epic,* discovered in the ruins of
Nineveh about the middle of the last century, to
the British Society of Biblical Archaeology on
December 3, 1872. This present publication may
thus be considered a centennial volume.

The first complete edition of the known cuneiform tablets was published in two volumes in 1884
and 1891 by Paul Haupt, and a two-volume tran-
scription and translation into German was made by

Peter Jensen in 1900 and 1901. Since then studies have so burgeoned that major publications concerned with the *Gilgamesh* story now number nearly three hundred, and Gilgamesh is finding his place in contemporary studies of world literature. The stories about him owe their appeal both to their poetic imagery and to his adventurous drive and tragic search for an immortality that finally eluded him and left him, in the end, inspecting and rejoicing in the walls of his own city, Uruk (biblical Erech).

Stories about Gilgamesh were popular among the Sumerians in the third millennium B.C., where the hero was celebrated as an exemplary ruler, human being, and hunter. Hundreds of years later, Babylonian scribes of Hammurapi's era (ca. 1750) repeated and revised these stories, and probably by Kassite times (ca. 1250) they were worked into the epic that was preserved in Assurbanipal's library on twelve tablets, now fragmentary, which today rest in the British Museum. Copies of the epic have been discovered at Megiddo (Palestine), Ugarit (Syria), and Boghazköy (Turkey) where translations from Akkadian into Hittite and Hurrian have also been found. Fragments dating from the Neo-Babylonian era (ca. 550 B.C.) attest continuing Mesopotamian scribal interest in the epic. A history of oral traditions about Gilgamesh should probably be assumed, though little more than that can at the present time be suggested.[2]

It has been argued, nevertheless, that however widespread the interest in Gilgamesh elsewhere, the epic was little known in Mesopotamia proper.[3] We do not yet know with certainty, for example, the complete *Gilgamesh* story, nor are we able to construct its textual history even provisionally. Passages from it that to us seem memorable were not quoted in other Mesopotamian texts, nor were the events it relates incorporated in any way into the other literature. Outside Mesopotamia, on the other hand, parallels are numerous. This argument, while it presents pertinent information, does not do justice to the Mesopotamian texts that have been preserved, and one can conclude at best that the Mesopotamian literary tradition is still not so well known that one can assess with confidence the role of Gilgamesh in it.

The epic seems to be rooted in history, though its incidents are certainly legendary. The Sumerian King List,[4] which names most of the Sumerian kings together with the lengths of their rule from the beginning "after kingship had descended from heaven" to the end of the third millennium, includes Gilgamesh as the fifth king of Uruk. The precise historical value of this King List is still not certainly known, though the historical framework it provides for Sumerian history is generally accepted. The reigns ascribed to the antediluvian kings (eight kings of five cities ruled a total of 241,200 years) and to the twenty-three kings of the first dynasty of Kish after the Flood (23 kings reigned 24,510 years, 3 months, 3½ days!) are even more fantastic than the lifetimes ascribed in the Bible to the first men before Abraham (Genesis 5). If one discounts the legendary lengths of rule, however, and assumes that some of those early rulers were contemporaries, one can discern in the List a conception of a time when some Sumerian political unity was probably achieved under the leadership of the city Kish. Gilgamesh of Uruk is assigned a reign of 126 years in the List, and in spite of its unrealistic length, now that archaeological discovery has confirmed the existence of his contemporary rulers in Kish and Ur, the fact of his reign cannot be doubted, though contemporary records of it are still to be found.[5] Some have sought hidden significance in the number 126 itself.

Although Gilgamesh was a Sumerian king, and five known Sumerian stories celebrated events of his career (Gilgamesh and the Bull of Heaven; the Death of Gilgamesh; Gilgamesh and Agga of Kish; Gilgamesh and the Land of the Living; Gilgamesh, Enkidu and the Nether World),[6] the Sumerians did not unify the material into a single narrative. Most of the elements in the later epic originated with the Sumerians, but their combination into the unified story necessitated their transformation. Enkidu, for example, was transformed from Gilgamesh's loyal servant in the Sumerian account to his beloved equal and friend in the Babylonian. On the other hand, some elements in the Sumerian tradition were dropped from the Babylonian. The twelfth tablet found at Nineveh probably did not belong to the Babylonian version but contained the final part of another Sumerian Gilgamesh tale, "Gilgamesh and the Huluppu-Tree." The epic thus appears to have been a Babylonian creation inspired by the search for an answer to questions about the goal of human existence. The story seems to have been revised and augmented from time to time until it probably received its final form toward the end of the second millennium, when the story of the great Flood may have been incorporated (the eleventh tablet from Nineveh). This latest version, containing more than three thousand lines, some of them incompletely preserved, lacks crucial parts of the story that thus far have been unrecovered, but it also provides help in understanding earlier fragments that otherwise would defy interpretation. The strong ties of friendship between Gilgamesh and Enkidu provide the foundation for the Babylonian epic, upon which the vain quest for the immortality of eternal youth and the troubled questions about life's goals are raised. This artistic unity and design were imposed on the material in Babylon.

The epic, as we know it from Assurbanipal's library, concerns the two divine-human heroes and inseparable friends, Gilgamesh and Enkidu, and the latter's death, which is the critical event in the story. Enkidu's fate is decided when he and Gilgamesh defeat and kill the monster Humbaba, and then kill the miraculous Bull of Heaven, capable of destroying three hundred men with a single snort of his fiery breath, which was afterward sent against them by the goddess, Ishtar. When the goddess, infuriated by the bull's death, cursed Gilgamesh for this deed, Enkidu hurled the dead bull's right thigh in her face with the taunt that he would gladly deal with her in the same way if he could. Thereafter the gods in council decree his death for reasons that were not accepted by all of them and remain obscure, and he dies. (The broken seventh tablet must have recorded the fact, since the eighth begins with Gilgamesh's lament over his friend's death.) That a demigod could die does not seem to have troubled the poet(s), and the conflict between the gods and their created superhuman beings may contain a clue, the significance of which eludes us, to the meaning of the epic. The biblical story of the Flood is introduced by a similar statement about demigods whose fate was sealed by the LORD. The rest of the epic tells how Gilgamesh searched in vain the world over to find an escape from death. Each time he was offered an escape he was unable to appropriate it effectively and was finally forced to give up the quest and return to Uruk.

The story has been described as a revolt against death, ending on a "jeering, unhappy, and unsatisfying" note. Defensible as that description certainly is, it scarcely does justice to the broad sweep and dramatic power of the poem and should be abandoned. Other universally appealing images and themes in the story have become common to our literary heritage: love, friendship, and loyalty; the way, the mountain, and the sea; all seeking to comprehend the incomprehensible mystery of human life. Next to them the revolt against death loses some of its force. Beginning and ending with a view of "ramparted Uruk" the story seems to emphasize a man's work as his glory and only hope for immortality. That hope may not have satisfied Gilgamesh, but with it he is forced to be content. Within that framework of human achievement the poem contains exquisite observations on human life and conduct that gently mock the heroic quest for escape from death, which is accepted as man's lot, his inevitable fate which should not be permitted to sour his joy in life. The following stanza is unsurpassed anywhere.

> Gilgamesh, whither rovest thou?
> The Life thou pursuest thou shalt not find.
> When the gods created mankind,
> Death for mankind they set aside,
> Life in their own hands retaining.
> Thou, Gilgamesh, let full be thy belly,

Make thou merry by day and by night.
Of each day make thou a feast of rejoicing,
Day and night dance thou and play!
Let thy garments be sparkling fresh,
Thy head be washed; bathe thou in water.
Pay heed to the little one that holds on to thy
    hand,
Let thy spouse delight in thy bosom!
For this is the task of mankind!

> X, iii   Old Babylonian Version,
> tr. E. A. Speiser

The legend of *Gilgamesh* in its seventh-century form was first translated into English hexameters in 1927 by R. Campbell Thompson of Oxford, who did his "utmost to preserve an absolutely literal translation."[7] His critical edition of the text, published two years later, is still a standard work in English. In 1946, Alexander Heidel of Chicago, in an effort to show the relationship between ancient Hebrew and Mesopotamian ideas about death, the afterlife, and the great Flood, published a new translation and discussion of the epic, which remains an essential aid to the study of the material.[8] The most recent English translations are the superb renderings of S. N. Kramer, who did the Sumerian texts, and E. A. Speiser, who did the Babylonian.[9]

Gilgamesh is not and should not be, however, the private preserve of scholars, and there have been laymen, sensitive to the power and charm of the epic, who relying on the work of specialists have introduced the story to a wider circle of readers. These men have sometimes been roundly condemned by the learned guardians of ancient lore, who pronounce their works of popularizing to be "painfully

123

inadequate." No one will deny that accurate texts and translations must perforce be prepared by experts, nor will anyone minimize the severe problems inherent in any work of translating, where the desired goal is not simply accurate rendering of words but authentic transmission of ideas. The so-called popularizers, at their best, seek to make available, for the world to enjoy, the ideas and artistic creations of the past that specialists have revealed; and who can doubt the worthiness of that purpose? Some of these popularizations are authentic, evocative, and worthy to be called artistic creations in their own right. Surely what a sensitive interpreter can do with an old story will not destroy the story but will give it a luminosity for which many yearn and are grateful. The *Epic of Gilgamesh* has inspired at least one novel by the same name, written by the young Swiss author Guido Bachmann, who heard in his own experience echoes of the ancient themes.

The first to attempt a free rendition of *Gilgamesh* in English was the professor of English, William E. Leonard. In collaboration with his friend, the German Egyptologist, Hermann Ranke, he "Englished" Ranke's German translation of *Gilgamesh* into what he then called "a rendering in free rhythms."[10] The usefulness and beauty of that work were immediately apparent, and it was widely used by students of literature. The present rendering by Herbert Mason is properly called a verse narrative. It is a sensitive, authentic retelling of the old story, an attempt to convey the profound anguish Gilgamesh suffered after his constant companion and friend, Enkidu, died. The author makes no claim to present an accurate rendering of the cuneiform text. He knows the ancient story well and tells it in the way it has become memorable to him. His narrative has its own spellbinding power, evoking feelings and thoughts familiar to all who suffer the loss of loved companions.

Mason's remarkable achievement is to offer this interpretation of *Gilgamesh* in a way that does no violence to the original, but rather concentrates its rays into an intense light on the central question about death. One who knows the ancient story is fascinated and moved by this account, which will also drive the novice to read the scholarly versions with new understanding. This rendering answers the unasked, personal question, What does Gilgamesh mean to me? with penetrating insight into the riddle of human life; and it leaves one asking of the story the same question for himself. To require of Mason more than that would be ungrateful.

Albert Schott remarked in the preface to his German translation of *Gilgamesh* that wanting to plumb its meaning is like seeking to understand the world.[11] We do not know what ancient tellers of this poignant tale intended. Authors like Herbert Mason help us find out.

NOTES

[1] S. N. Kramer, *The Sumerians*, Chicago 1964, p. 45, 185.
[2] Cf. W. G. Lambert, "The Historicity of Gilgamesh," in *Gilgamesh et sa légende*, ed. Paul Garelli, Paris 1960, p. 50.
[3] A. L. Oppenheim, *Ancient Mesopotamia*, Chicago 1964, p. 256.
[4] A. L. Oppenheim, in J. B. Pritchard, *Ancient Near Eastern Texts* (ANET) Princeton 1950, 3rd Ed. 1969, p. 265 f.; Kramer, *Op. cit.*, appendix E.
[5] Cf. Kramer in P. Garelli, *Op. cit.*, pp. 59–68.

[6] Cf. Kramer, *The Sumerians*, pp. 185–205; also in ANET pp. 44–52.

[7] *The Epic of Gilgamish*. A new translation from a collation of the cuneiform tablets in the British Museum rendered literally into English hexameters, London 1928.

[8] *The Gilgamesh Epic and Old Testament Parallels*, Chicago.

[9] In J. B. Pritchard, ANET.

[10] *Gilgamesh. Epic of Old Babylonia*, New York 1934.

[11] A. Schott, *Das Gilgamesh-Epos neu übersetzt und mit Anmerkungen versehen*, rev. by W. von Soden, Stuttgart 1970 (Reclams Universalbibliothek 7235/35a).

Afterword to the Mariner Edition

My instinctive response to the story of *Gilgamesh* has always been to two of its principal themes: friendship and loss. For me, everything in the epic leads to and out of these experiences. The connection between them engaged me once to look back at my own life, at history, at reality divested of formal religious revelation, philosophical reflection, and academic knowledge. I was put by its story-power into a kind of pre-conscious, pre-learned, pre-judgmental state. Two men, first fighting, then befriending, one facing death, the other the pain of loss, the survivor's embarking on an impossible journey to find eternal life, only to lose what he was given to a serpent, was a relentlessly poignant, tragic story stripped bare of illusions and spiritual hope, yet in its hero's defiance of death it revealed a nobility of soul inherent in our human condition.

The depth of loss, the resounding voice of grief, became a comfort to me and has remained so: an unexpected ancient companion to my own fragmented story. But this isn't all that the tale is about. There's the relationship of gods to humanity, the sacredness of the walled citadel to be maintained by the king, the politics of the elders, the social structuring, the position of women, the kindredness of animal and man and all of nature to humanity, nature's animateness and plenitude, justice and injustice, the cross-vitalization between city and steppe, the boundaries between the lawful and the forbidden, the effect of all these on the two friends, and of course history.

One can adapt, as several authors have done, certain parts to the exclusion of other parts, emphasizing the grandly heroic as opposed to human vulnerability, for instance. Also, because of the presence of the flood story, so close in detail to the later biblical account but so different in spirit, one might regard this as a religious narrative centered on the quest for eternal life and on the quasi-prophetic figure of Utnapishtim, who was chosen with his wife to build the ark and with the selected animals to survive the divinely ordered devastation. In the ancient Near East I believe such a reading is cautiously justifiable, given that region's abundant succession of cultures and assimilative power of myths and religious configurations. While I suggested a compassionate One, humanly hoped for beyond all the irresponsible, uncompassionate gods, my retelling was in no way theological in intent or spirit, but emphatically human in its depictions of aspirations and sufferings and in its naked, essential understanding of reality.

For me, friendship and loss formed the delicate yet enduring chain that linked together the various pearls presented episodically throughout the story. Hence my constant echoes of the one and repeated foreshadowings of the other.

As regards the role of personal experience in the retelling of such a story, I believe that *Gilgamesh* came to me out of a void I perceived early in my life. The power of myth was felt in its unexpected ambush of reality itself as I knew it. Its narrative form called for immediacy of response and simplicity of style. And though the passion to respond became coupled with the need to understand its meaning, the latter remained hidden within the former, the telling of which was paramount.

HERBERT MASON, DECEMBER 2002